BUILDING BLOCKS OF PHYSICAL SCIENCE

# MATTER AND ITS PROPERTIES

Written by Joseph Midthun

Illustrated by Samuel Hiti

a Scott Fetzer company
Chicago

World Book, Inc.
180 North LaSalle Street
Suite 900
Chicago, Illinois 60601
USA

For information about other World Book publications, visit our website at **www.worldbook.com** or call **1-800-WORLDBK (967-5325)**.
For information about sales to schools and libraries, call 1-800-975-3250 (United States), or 1-800-837-5365 (Canada).



Library of Congress Cataloging-in-Publication Data for this volume has been applied for.

Building Blocks of Physical Science
ISBN: 978-0-7166-4460-6 (set, hc.)

Matter and Its Properties
ISBN: 978-0-7166-4469-9 (hc.)

Also available as:
ISBN: 978-0-7166-4479-8 (e-book)

1st printing March 2022



**Acknowledgments:**
Created by Samuel Hiti and Joseph Midthun
Art by Samuel Hiti
Additional art by David Shephard/The Bright Agency
Additional spot art by Dreamstime and Shutterstock
Text by Joseph Midthun

# TABLE OF CONTENTS



There is a glossary on page 39. Terms defined in the glossary are in type **that looks like this** on their first appearance.

WHAT IS MATTER?
Hi!
I'm MATTER.
Everything in the world is made of me!

The ground under your feet is made of matter.

The water in a river is made of matter.

The clouds above you are made of matter.

The stars in the sky are made of matter.

Even *you* are made of matter.

Matter is anything that has **mass** and **volume**.
MASS
VOLUME

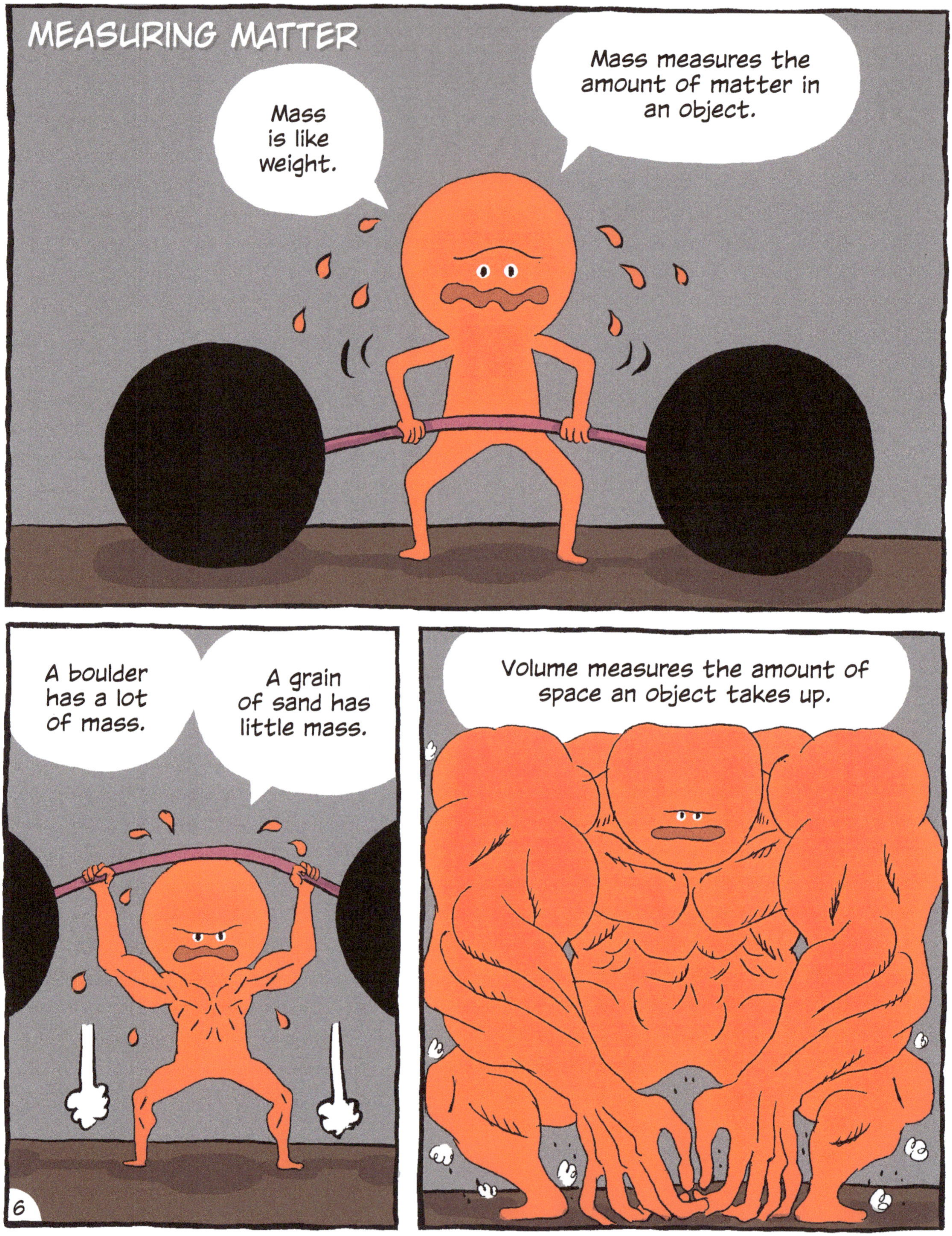

## MEASURING MATTER

Mass is like weight.

Mass measures the amount of matter in an object.

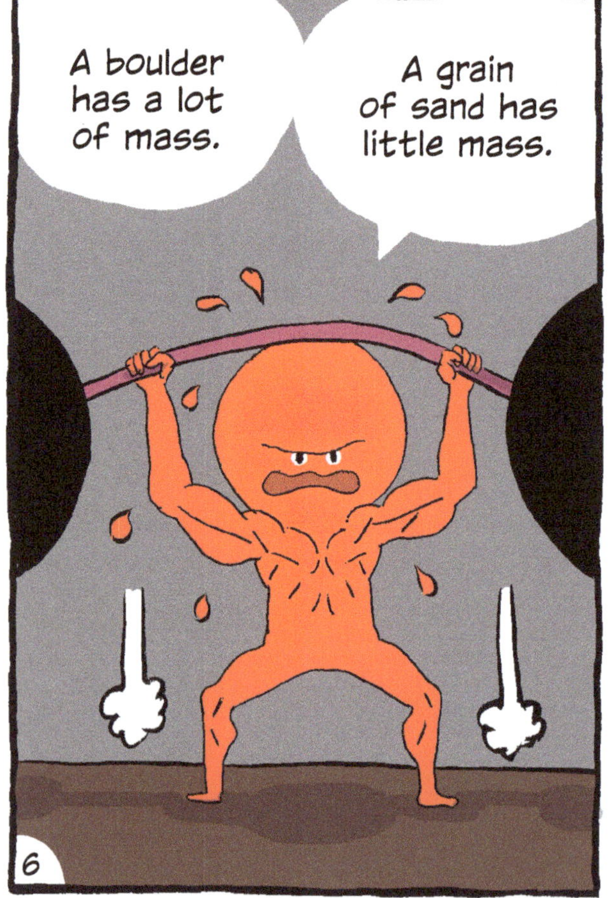


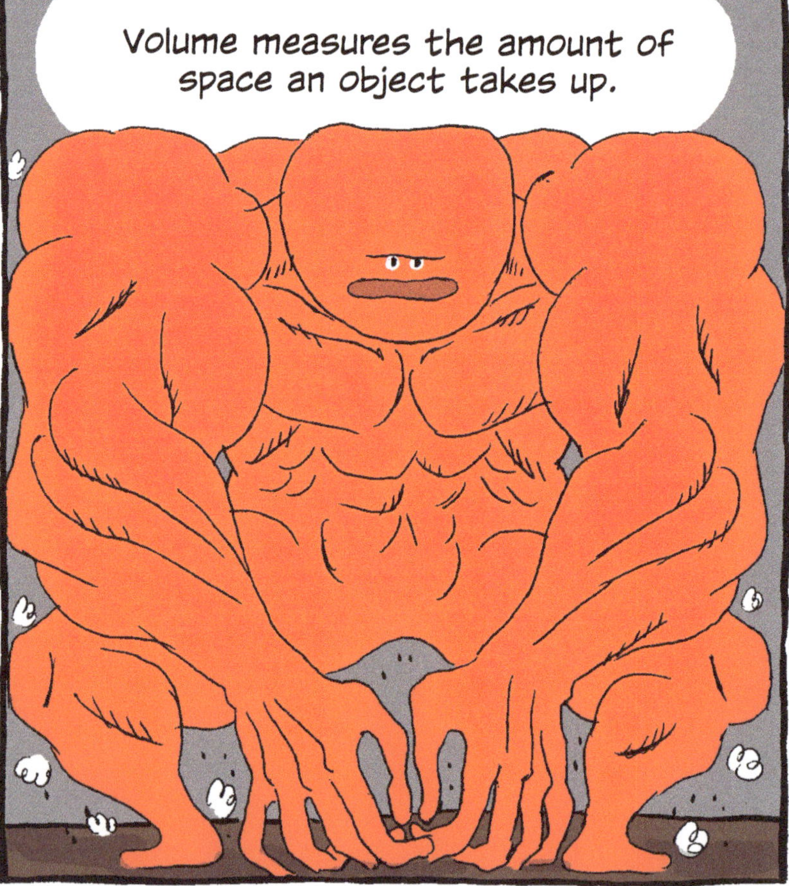

For example, take a bowling ball and a balloon.
The bowling ball has more mass than the balloon.

But they both take up about the same amount of space.
They have similar volume. How can this be?

The bowling ball packs more mass into the same amount of space.

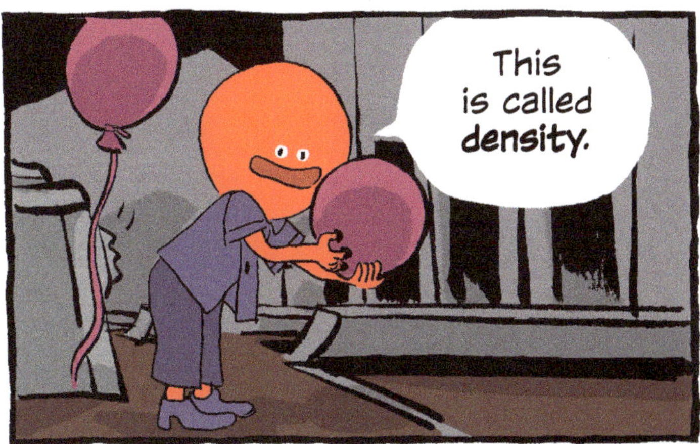
This is called **density.**

Density measures how much matter is in a certain space.
The bowling ball is more dense than the balloon.
Strike!
CRASH
SWOOP

COLOR

TEXTURE

SHAPE

SIZE

These pages show examples of some properties of matter you can see or feel.

...if it is **attracted** to magnets.

...if it dissolves in a liquid.
...how easily it melts, freezes, or changes into a gas.

# A LOOK INSIDE

But what is matter *really* made of?

Let's take a look inside!

ZAP!

I'm made of **molecules**!
Molecules are made up of **atoms**–tiny particles.

Atoms are the basic units of matter.
Look even closer.

Atoms have a **nucleus**, or center.

**Protons** and **neutrons** are tiny particles inside the nucleus.

**Electrons** are even tinier particles that move around the nucleus.

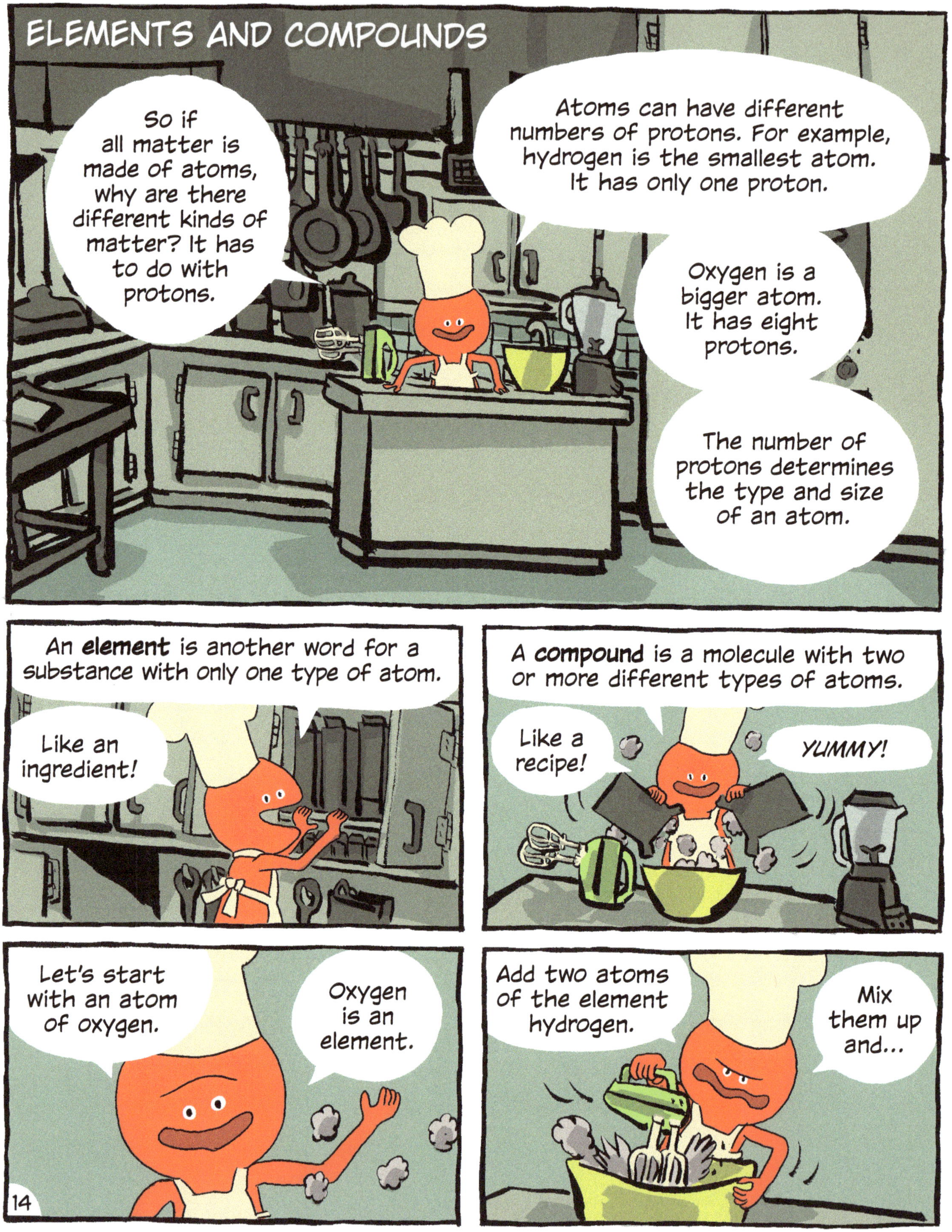

# ELEMENTS AND COMPOUNDS

So if all matter is made of atoms, why are there different kinds of matter? It has to do with protons.

Atoms can have different numbers of protons. For example, hydrogen is the smallest atom. It has only one proton.

Oxygen is a bigger atom. It has eight protons.

The number of protons determines the type and size of an atom.

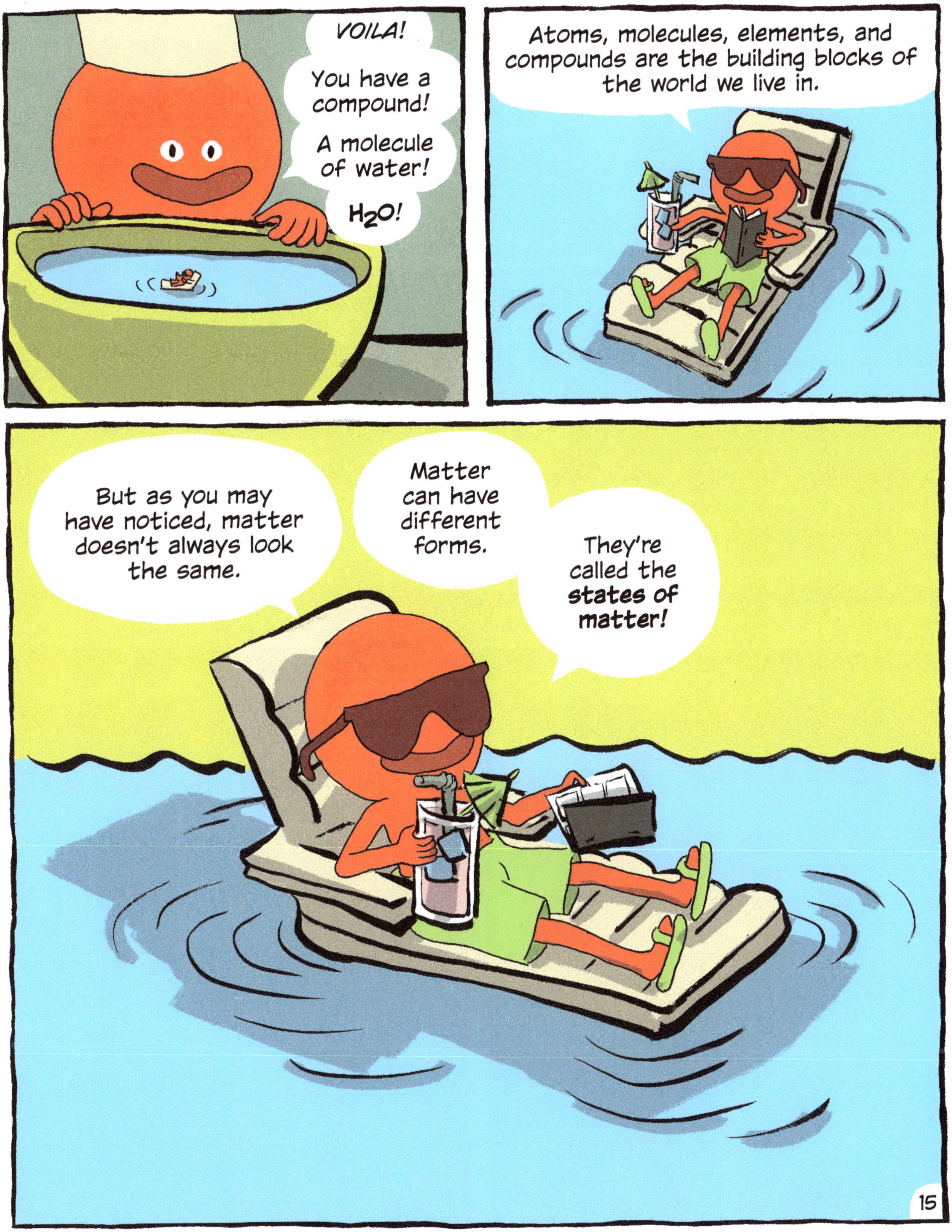

But as you may have noticed, matter doesn't always look the same.

Matter can have different forms.

They're called the **states of matter!**

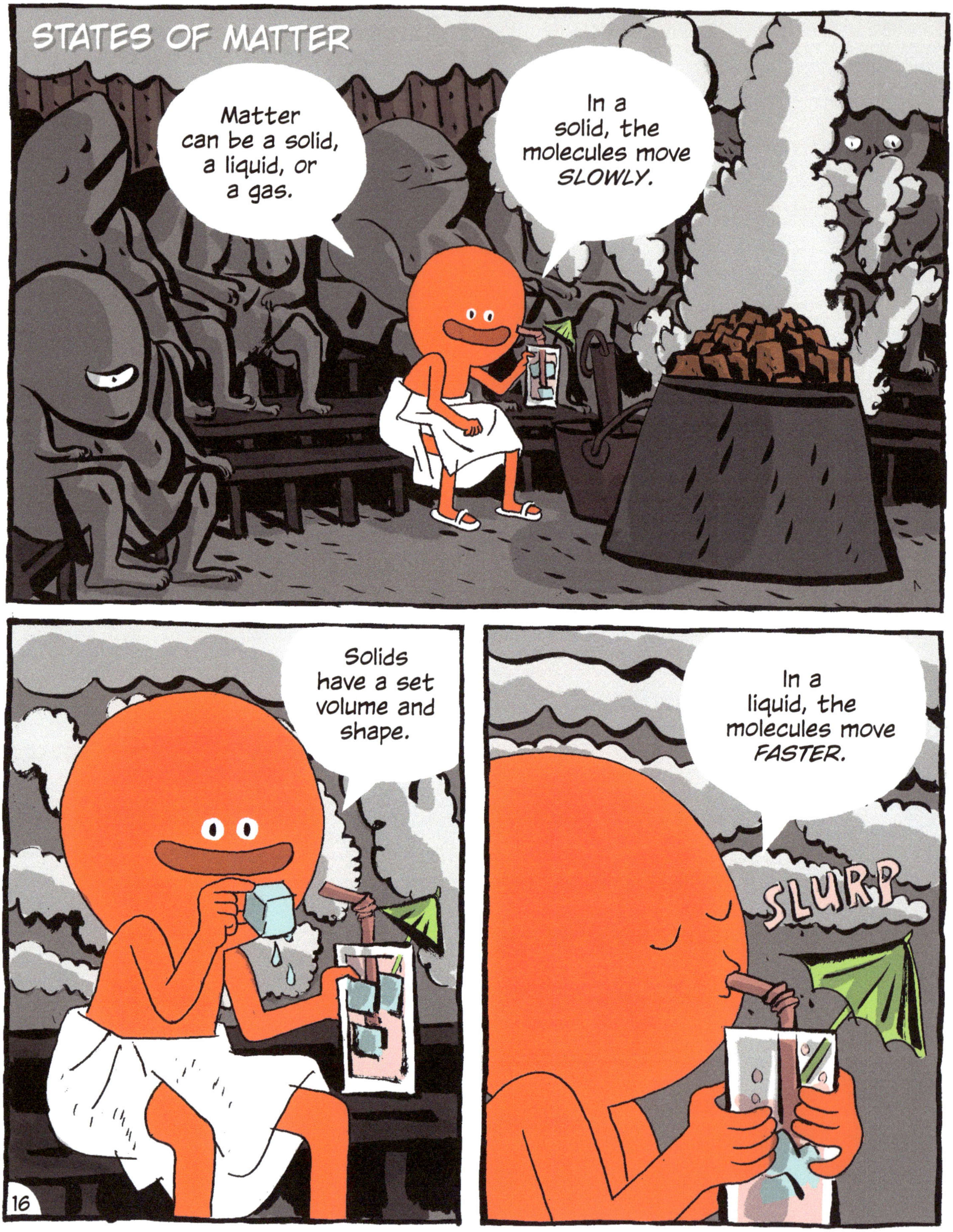

# STATES OF MATTER

Matter can be a solid, a liquid, or a gas.

In a solid, the molecules move *SLOWLY.*

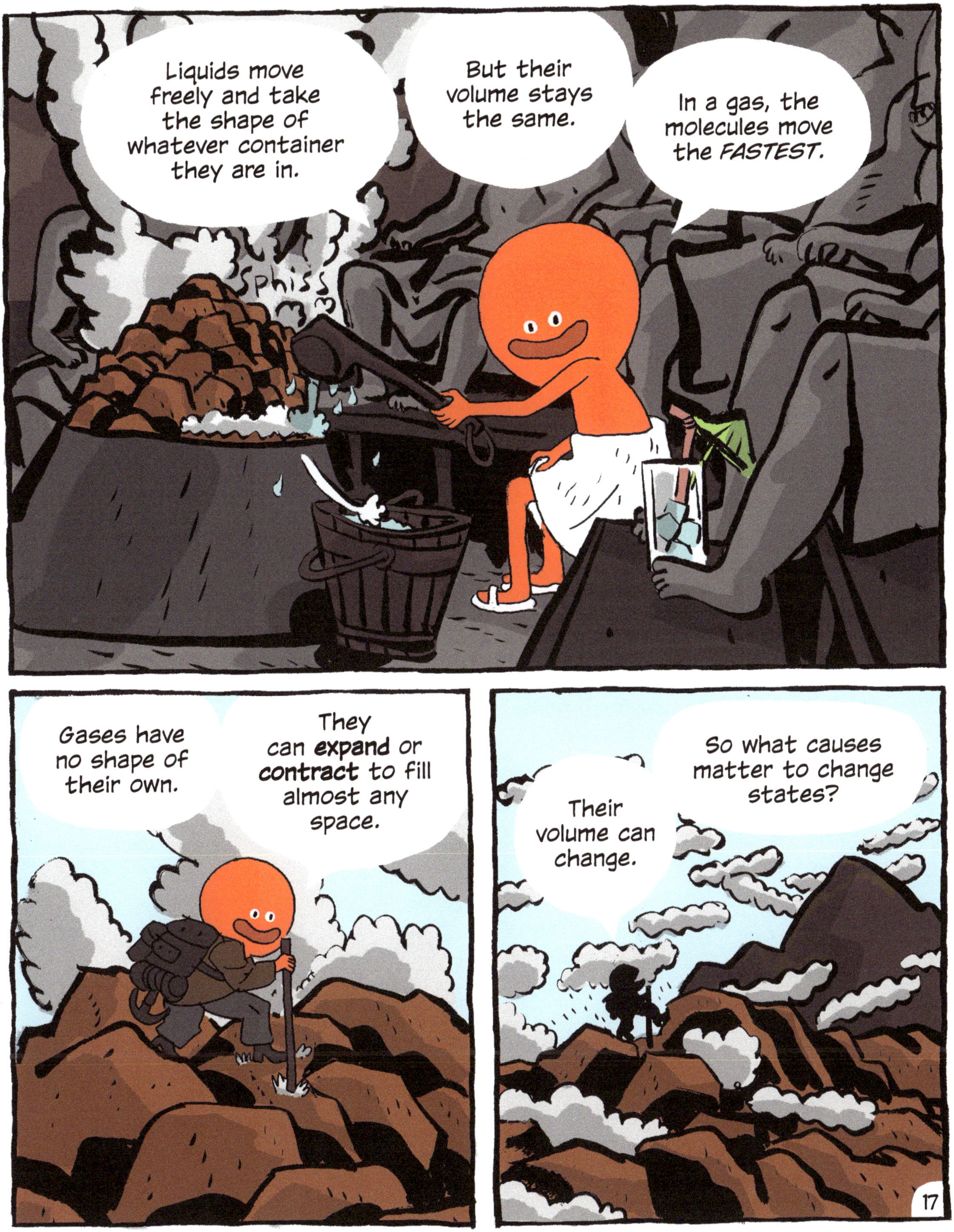

Liquids move freely and take the shape of whatever container they are in.

But their volume stays the same.

In a gas, the molecules move the *FASTEST*.

Sphiss

ENERGY!

Energy has the ability to cause change.

Heat is a form of energy. Heat can melt solid rock into lava by causing the molecules that make up the rock to move faster.

When the molecules move faster, they slide past one another.

They've become a liquid!

When the liquid gets hot enough, the molecules break free from one another.

They are now a gas!

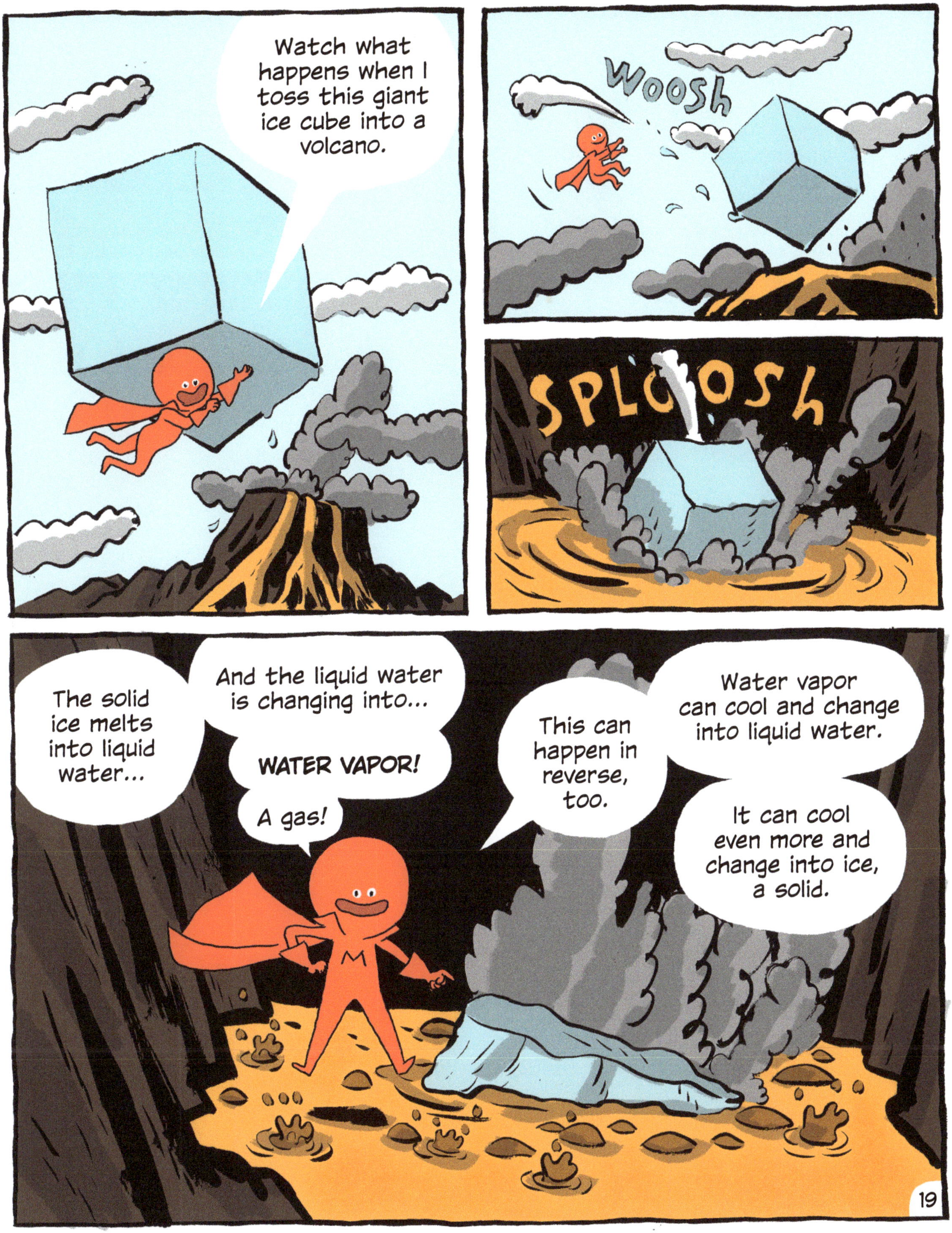

The solid ice melts into liquid water...

And the liquid water is changing into...

**WATER VAPOR!**

A gas!

This can happen in reverse, too.

Water vapor can cool and change into liquid water.

It can cool even more and change into ice, a solid.

## GROUPING MATTER

As you have seen, not all matter is the same.

Scientists group almost all elements of matter into two categories:

**Metals** and **nonmetals.**

Metals are a huge group of elements.

They often appear shiny because they reflect light well.

Copper, gold, iron, lead, mercury, silver, and tin are examples of metals.

HOP
All metals are solids at room temperature *except* mercury, which is a liquid.
The atoms in most metals are closer together than the atoms in nonmetals.
This makes metals more dense.

Metals can be shaped into useful objects.
They can be hammered into thin sheets without breaking.

They can be drawn into wires.

Most metals are also good **conductors** of heat and electricity.

This is why electric wires are made of metal.

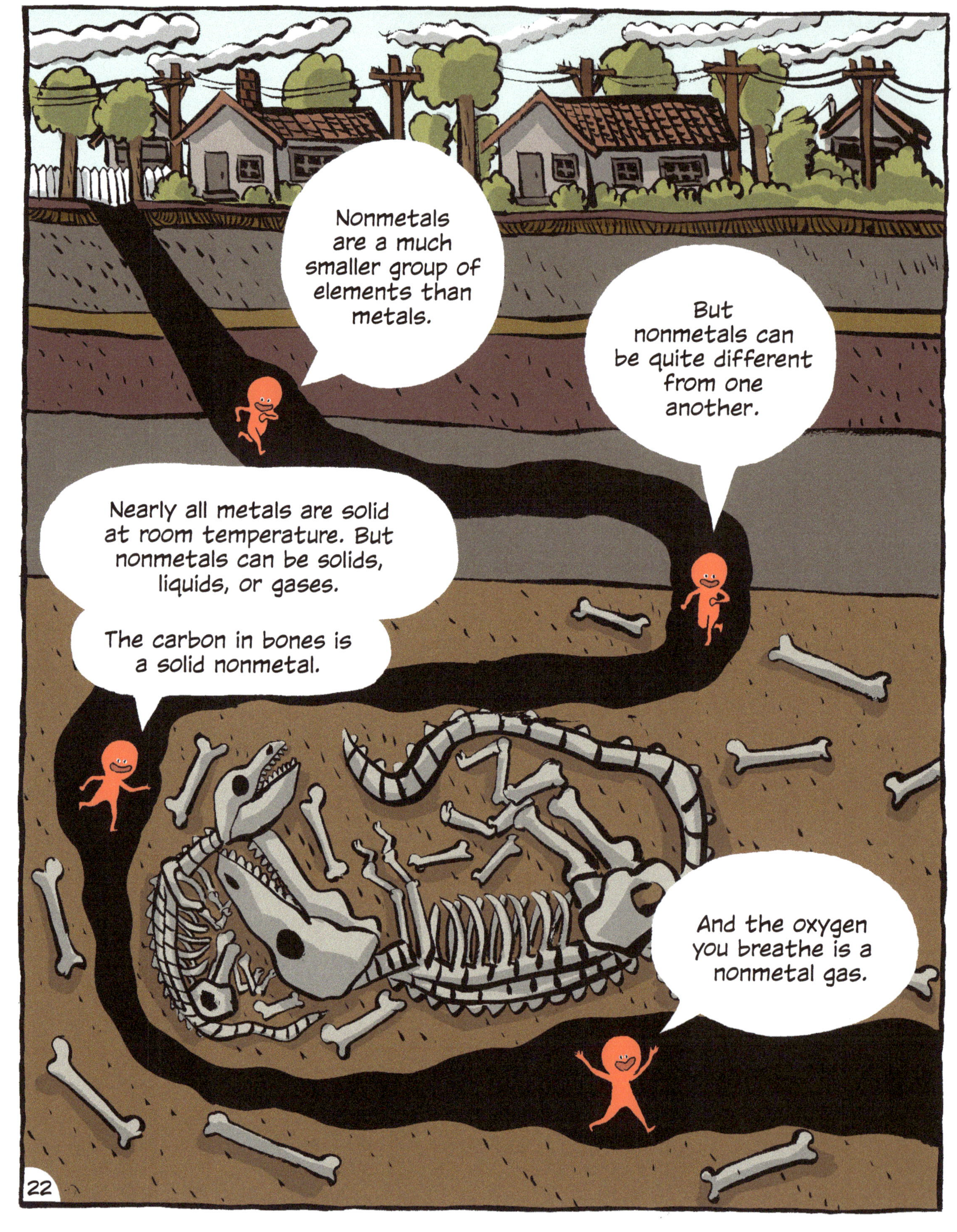
Nonmetals are a much smaller group of elements than metals.
But nonmetals can be quite different from one another.
Nearly all metals are solid at room temperature. But nonmetals can be solids, liquids, or gases.
The carbon in bones is a solid nonmetal.
And the oxygen you breathe is a nonmetal gas.

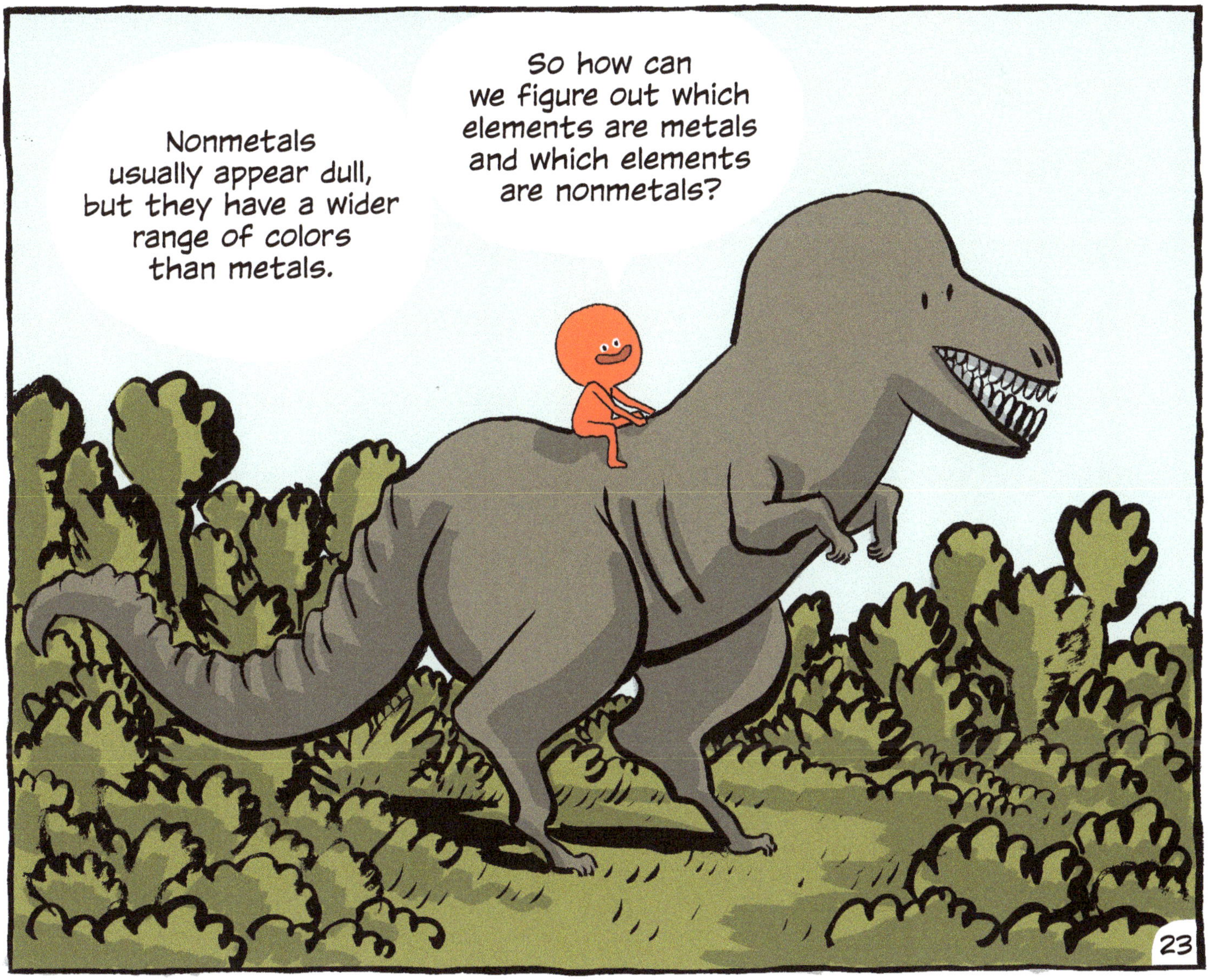

Nonmetals usually appear dull, but they have a wider range of colors than metals.

So how can we figure out which elements are metals and which elements are nonmetals?

# THE PERIODIC TABLE

The **periodic table** lists all the elements that scientists have identified so far.

Metals are on one side of the table and nonmetals, except hydrogen, are on the other side.

Each element has its own symbol. Remember when we made a molecule of water?

I called it $H_2O$.

Here's why!

| | 1 | 2 | 3 | 4 | 5 | 6 | 7 | 8 | 9 – |
|---|---|---|---|---|---|---|---|---|---|
| 1 | 1<br>**H**<br>Hydrogen | | | | | | | | |
| 2 | 3<br>**Li**<br>Lithium | 4<br>**Be**<br>Beryllium | | | | | | | |
| 3 | 11<br>**Na**<br>Sodium | 12<br>**Mg**<br>Magnesium | | | | | | | |
| 4 | 19<br>**K**<br>Potassium | 20<br>**Ca**<br>Calcium | 21<br>**Sc**<br>Scandium | 22<br>**Ti**<br>Titanium | 23<br>**V**<br>Vanadium | 24<br>**Cr**<br>Chromium | 25<br>**Mn**<br>Manganese | 26<br>**Fe**<br>Iron | 27<br>**Co**<br>Cobal |
| 5 | 37<br>**Rb**<br>Rubidium | 38<br>**Sr**<br>Strontium | 39<br>**Y**<br>Yttrium | 40<br>**Zr**<br>Zirconium | 41<br>**Nb**<br>Niobium | 42<br>**Mo**<br>Molybdenum | 43<br>**Tc**<br>Technetium | 44<br>**Ru**<br>Ruthenium | 45<br>**Rh**<br>Rhodiu |
| 6 | 55<br>**Cs**<br>Cesium | 56<br>**Ba**<br>Barium | | 72<br>**Hf**<br>Hafnium | 73<br>**Ta**<br>Tantalum | 74<br>**W**<br>Tungsten | 75<br>**Re**<br>Rhenium | 76<br>**Os**<br>Osmium | 77<br>**Ir**<br>Iridiu |
| 7 | 87<br>**Fr**<br>Francium | 88<br>**Ra**<br>Radium | | 104<br>**Rf**<br>Rutherfordium | 105<br>**Db**<br>Dubnium | 106<br>**Sg**<br>Seaborgium | 107<br>**Bh**<br>Bohrium | 108<br>**Hs**<br>Hassium | 109<br>**Mt**<br>Meitneri |

| 57<br>**La**<br>Lanthanum | 58<br>**Ce**<br>Cerium | 59<br>**Pr**<br>Praseodymium | 60<br>**Nd**<br>Neodymium | 61<br>**Pm**<br>Promethium | 62<br>**Sm**<br>Samarium | 63<br>**Eu**<br>Europiu |
|---|---|---|---|---|---|---|
| 89<br>**Ac**<br>Actinium | 90<br>**Th**<br>Thorium | 91<br>**Pa**<br>Protactinium | 92<br>**U**<br>Uranium | 93<br>**Np**<br>Neptunium | 94<br>**Pu**<br>Plutonium | 95<br>**Am**<br>Americiu |

You can read the table like this...

Atomic Number
Atomic Symbol
Atomic Name

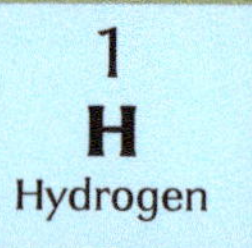

The symbol for hydrogen is *H*—get it?

"H" for *hydrogen*.

"O" for *oxygen*.

So the symbol for a molecule of water, two hydrogen atoms and one oxygen atom, is $H_2O$!

| 10 | 11 | 12 | 13 | 14 | 15 | 16 | 17 | 18 |
|---|---|---|---|---|---|---|---|---|
| | | | | | | | | 2 **He** Helium |
| | | | 5 **B** Boron | 6 **C** Carbon | 7 **N** Nitrogen | 8 **O** Oxygen | 9 **F** Fluorine | 10 **Ne** Neon |
| | | | 13 **Al** Aluminum | 14 **Si** Silicon | 15 **P** Phosphorus | 16 **S** Sulfur | 17 **Cl** Chlorine | 18 **Ar** Argon |
| 28 **Ni** Nickel | 29 **Cu** Copper | 30 **Zn** Zinc | 31 **Ga** Gallium | 32 **Ge** Germanium | 33 **As** Arsenic | 34 **Se** Selenium | 35 **Br** Bromine | 36 **Kr** Krypton |
| 46 **Pd** Palladium | 47 **Ag** Silver | 48 **Cd** Cadmium | 49 **In** Indium | 50 **Sn** Tin | 51 **Sb** Antimony | 52 **Te** Tellurium | 53 **I** Iodine | 54 **Xe** Xenon |
| 78 **Pt** Platinum | 79 **Au** Gold | 80 **Hg** Mercury | 81 **Tl** Thallium | 82 **Pb** Lead | 83 **Bi** Bismuth | 84 **Po** Polonium | 85 **At** Astatine | 86 **Rn** Radon |
| 110 **Ds** rmstadtium | 111 **Rg** Roentgenium | 112 **Cn** Copernicium | 113 **Nh** Nihonium | 114 **Fl** Flerovium | 115 **Mc** Moscovium | 116 **Lv** Livermorium | 117 **Ts** Tennessine | 118 **Og** Oganesson |

| | | | | | | | |
|---|---|---|---|---|---|---|---|
| 64 **Gd** adolinium | 65 **Tb** Terbium | 66 **Dy** Dysprosium | 67 **Ho** Holmium | 68 **Er** Erbium | 69 **Tm** Thulium | 70 **Yb** Ytterbium | 71 **Lu** Lutetium |
| 96 **Cm** Curium | 97 **Bk** Berkelium | 98 **Cf** Californium | 99 **Es** Einsteinium | 100 **Fm** Fermium | 101 **Md** Mendelevium | 102 **No** Nobelium | 103 **Lr** Lawrencium |

Metals | Metalloids | Nonmetals

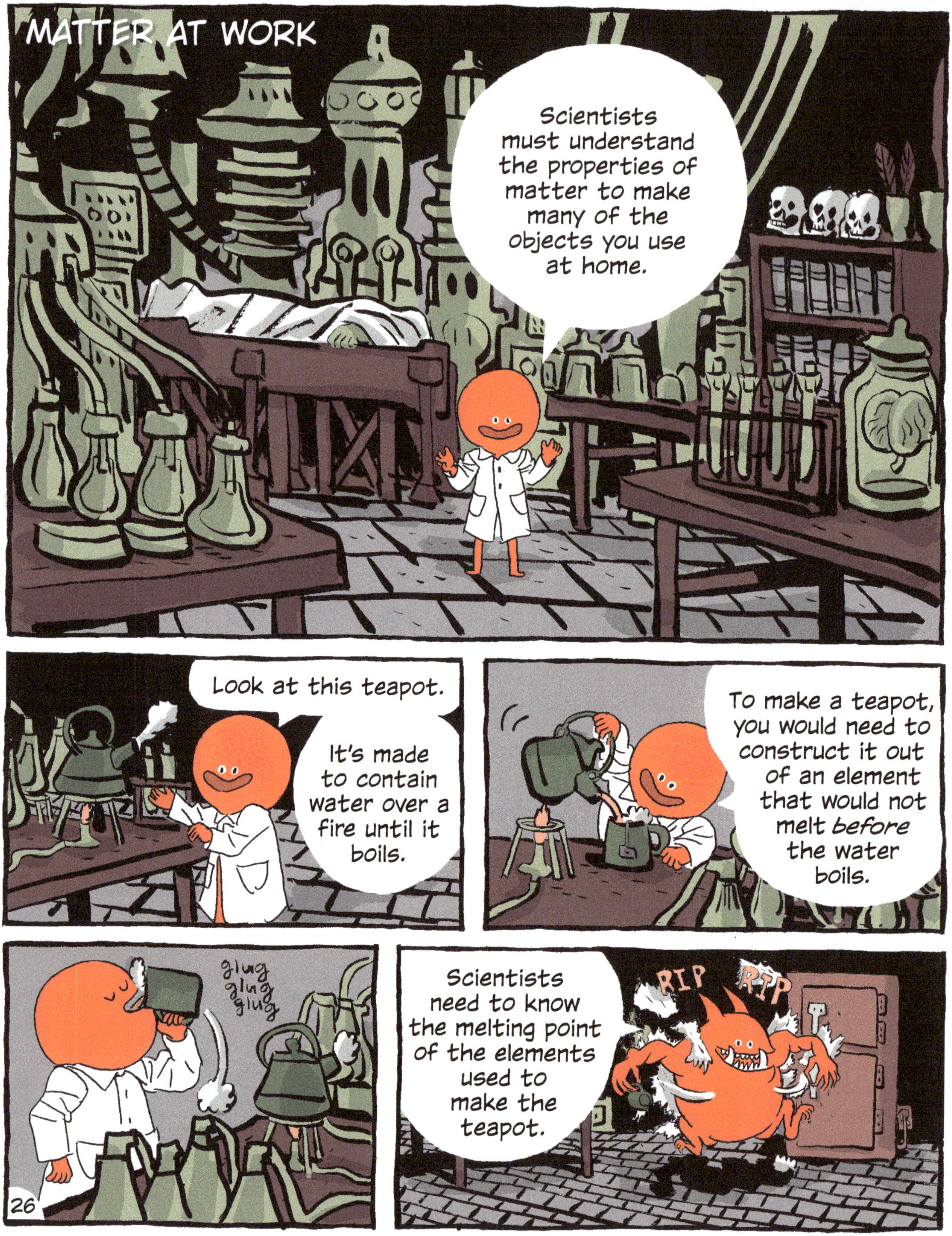

# MATTER AT WORK

Scientists must understand the properties of matter to make many of the objects you use at home.

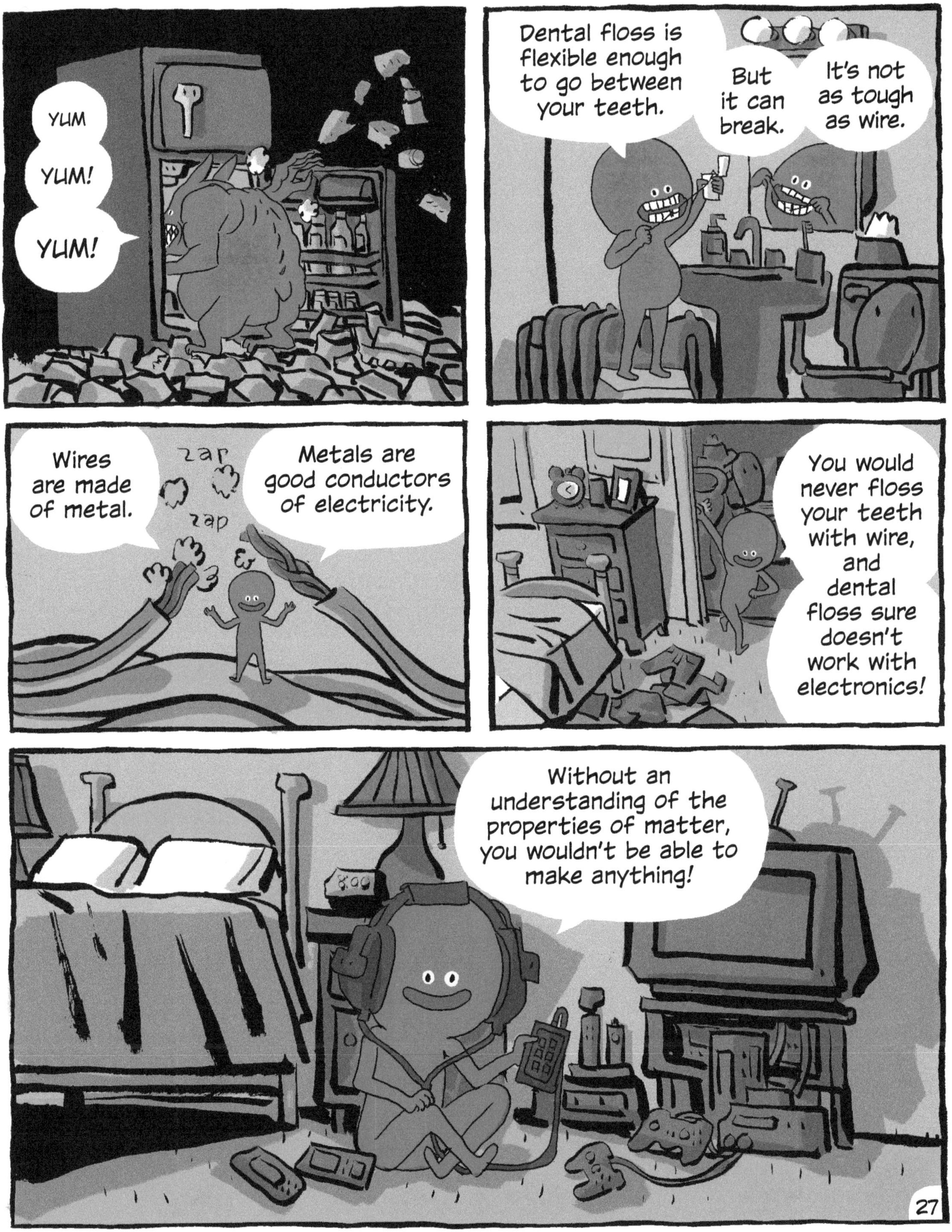

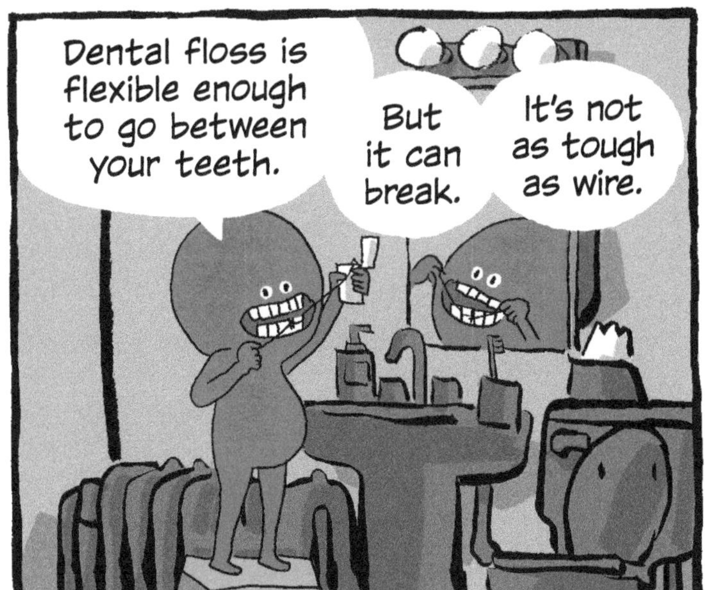

Without an understanding of the properties of matter, you wouldn't be able to make anything!

MATTER, MATTER, EVERYWHERE!
Now that you've learned about matter, you'll never look at the world the same way!
How many different kinds of matter do you see in this picture?
Can you spot the metals and nonmetals?
What about solids, liquids, and gases?
Hi!

Everything you use in your everyday life is made of matter.
Too often, humans take matter for granted.
Next time something catches your eye, see if you can notice *ME* in it!
I'm ***MATTER!***
Bye!

# TIMELINE

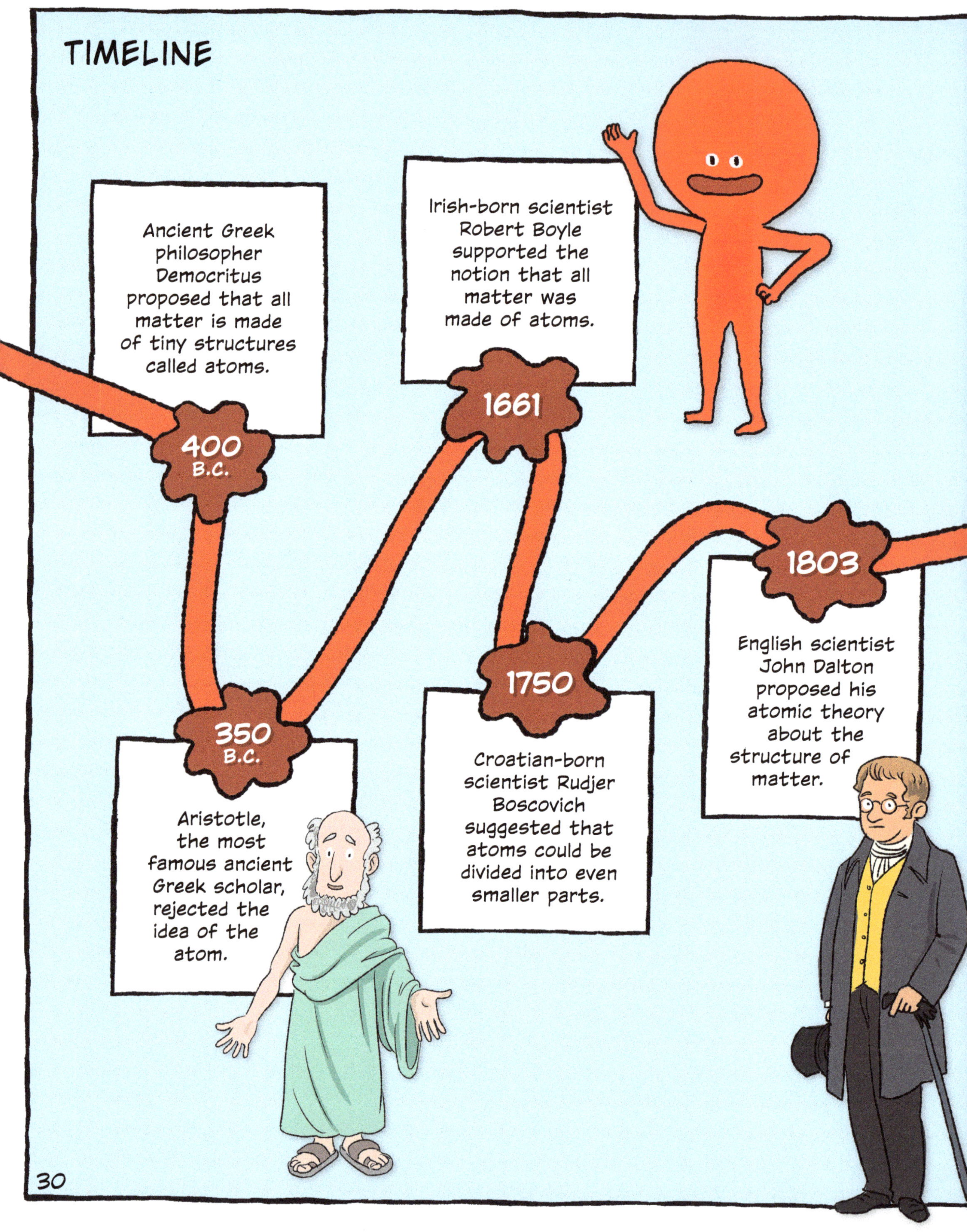

400 B.C.
Ancient Greek philosopher Democritus proposed that all matter is made of tiny structures called atoms.
350 B.C.
Aristotle, the most famous ancient Greek scholar, rejected the idea of the atom.
1661
Irish-born scientist Robert Boyle supported the notion that all matter was made of atoms.
1750
Croatian-born scientist Rudjer Boscovich suggested that atoms could be divided into even smaller parts.
1803
English scientist John Dalton proposed his atomic theory about the structure of matter.

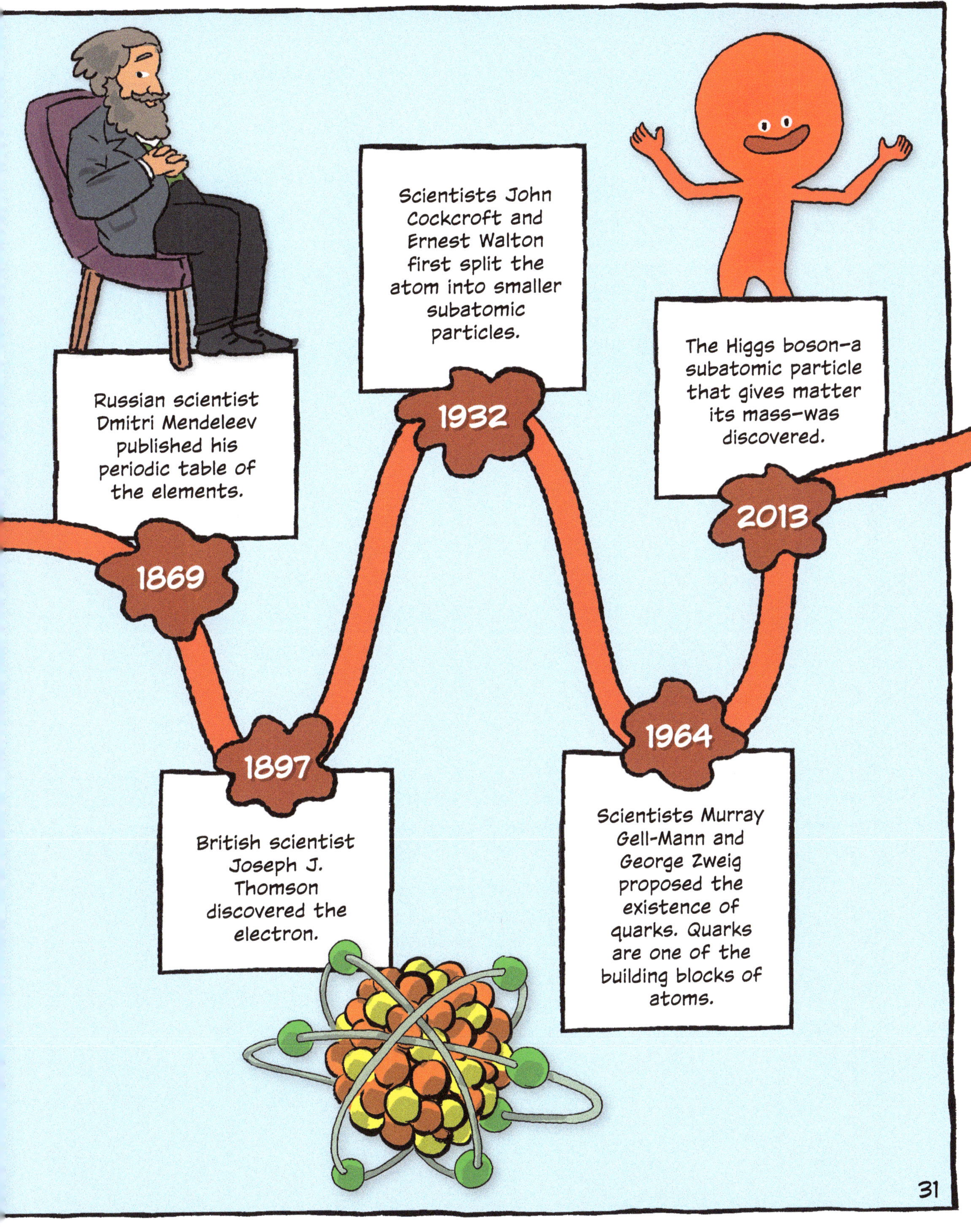
1869
Russian scientist Dmitri Mendeleev published his periodic table of the elements.
1897
British scientist Joseph J. Thomson discovered the electron.
1932
Scientists John Cockcroft and Ernest Walton first split the atom into smaller subatomic particles.
1964
Scientists Murray Gell-Mann and George Zweig proposed the existence of quarks. Quarks are one of the building blocks of atoms.
2013
The Higgs boson—a subatomic particle that gives matter its mass—was discovered.

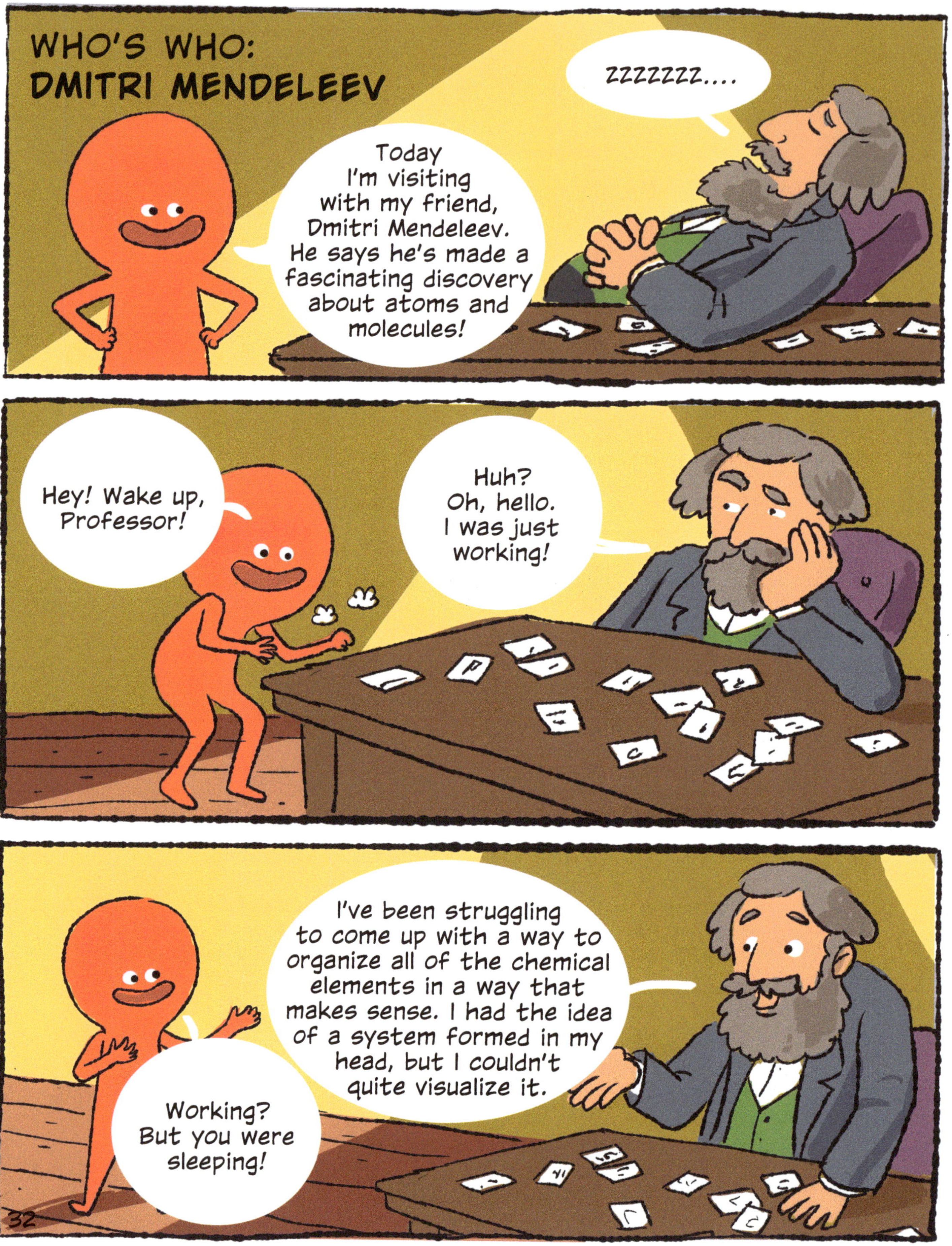

# WHO'S WHO:
# DMITRI MENDELEEV

Today I'm visiting with my friend, Dmitri Mendeleev. He says he's made a fascinating discovery about atoms and molecules!

ZZZZZZZ....

Sounds exhausting!

It was! Then, in a dream, a table where all the elements fell into proper place appeared to me! I immediately wrote it down on a piece of paper when I woke up.

## Fact File

**Name:** Dmitri Ivanovich Mendeleev

**Born:** 1834 in Tobolsk, Russia

**Occupation:** Chemist

**Claim to fame:** Mendeleev's dream led to the *periodic table*, a chart arranging all the chemical elements. The periodic table ranks as one of the most useful tools in chemistry ever invented.

## CAN YOU BELIEVE IT?!

The word **atom** comes from a Greek word meaning "uncuttable." But scientists can now split atoms up into even smaller subatomic particles.

**The largest atom** known is that of the artificially created element oganesson. An atom of oganesson has 118 protons.

Adding other elements to **metals** can give them many useful properties. Steel is mostly iron with just a tiny amount of carbon added.

**Nonmetal** elements are pretty useful too! Carbon, oxygen, and hydrogen make up living things.

Nothing you can see is made up of a single atom. Most atoms are bonded to one or more other atoms in the form of **molecules.**

Much of the small amount of the metallic element iridium in Earth's crust came from **an asteroid** that struck the planet!

The densest objects in the universe are neutron stars. A small spoonful of material from a neutron star

**weighs millions of tons!**

Scientists use a unit called

**the mole**

to measure atoms and other small particles. One mole contains 602,214,085,700,000,000,000,000 objects.

A mole of water weighs just 0.6 ounce (18 grams).

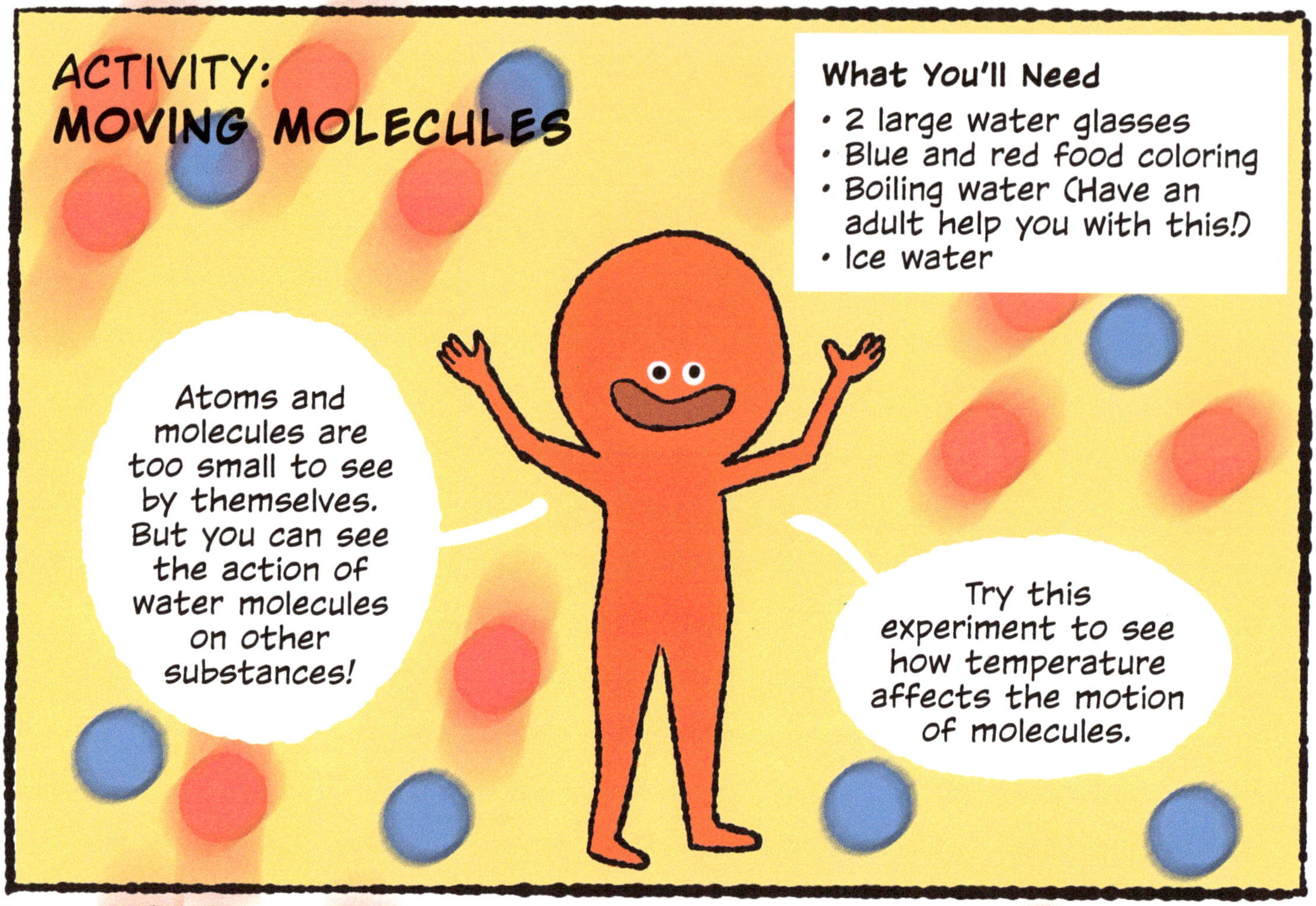

# ACTIVITY: MOVING MOLECULES

**What You'll Need**

- 2 large water glasses
- Blue and red food coloring
- Boiling water (Have an adult help you with this!)
- Ice water

Atoms and molecules are too small to see by themselves. But you can see the action of water molecules on other substances!

Try this experiment to see how temperature affects the motion of molecules.

Fill one glass with cold water and add some ice cubes. Let the water stand for a few minutes so that it gets well chilled. Then remove the ice cubes and let the cold water sit for another minute or so, until the water is still.

Add one drop of blue food coloring to the water. Watch how the color moves through the water.

Ask an adult to help you fill the second glass with water that has just boiled. Wait a few minutes until the hot water is still. Then add a drop of red food coloring to the hot water.
Watch how the color moves through the hot water. Was the speed and motion of the red coloring different from the way the blue coloring moved in the cold water?

Because they have more energy, the molecules of hot water are moving faster than the molecules of cold water.
This causes the red coloring to spread throughout the glass much faster compared with the blue coloring in the cold water.

## WORDS TO KNOW

**atom** one of the basic units of matter.

**attract** to pull one object toward another.

**compound** a substance that contains more than one kind of atom.

**conductor** something that allows heat, electricity, light, sound, or other form of energy to pass through it.

**contract** to decrease in size.

**density** the amount of matter in a particular volume of a substance.

**electron** a kind of particle that circles around the nucleus (center) of an atom. Electrons have a negative electric charge.

**element** a substance made of only one kind of atom.

**expand** to increase in size.

**mass** the amount of matter in an object.

**matter** what all things are made of.

**metal** any of a large group of elements that includes copper, gold, iron, lead, silver, tin, and other elements that share similar qualities.

**molecule** two or more atoms chemically bonded together.

**neutron** a kind of particle inside the nucleus (center) of an atom. Neutrons have no electric charge.

**nonmetal** materials that do not have the properties of metals. Wood, glass, plastic, and rock are examples of nonmetals.

**nucleus** the center of an atom. Protons and neutrons are inside the nucleus.

**periodic table** a chart that lists the known chemical elements arranged according to their characteristics.

**property** quality or power belonging specially to something.

**proton** a kind of particle inside the nucleus (center) of an atom. Protons have a positive electric charge.

**states of matter** the different forms of matter. The most familiar are solid, liquid, and gas.

**volume** the amount of space something takes up.

**water vapor** water in the state of a gas.

# INDEX

www.ingramcontent.com/pod-product-compliance
Ingram Content Group UK Ltd.
Pitfield, Milton Keynes, MK11 3LW, UK
UKHW061957290726
14090UKWH00021B/1261

9 780716 650621